SPOTLIGHT ON GLOBAL ISSUES

PROTECTING
EARTH'S LAND

Daniel R. Faust

ROSEN
PUBLISHING

NEW YORK

Published in 2022 by The Rosen Publishing Group, Inc.
29 East 21st Street, New York, NY 10010

First Edition

Editor: Theresa Emminizer
Book Design: Michael Flynn

Photo Credits: Cover Marius Dobilas/Shutterstock.com; (series globe background) photastic/Shutterstock.com; p. 5 (all) Jeremie Richard/AFP/Getty Images; p. 6 Thammanoon Khamchalee/Shutterstock.com; p. 7 Joao Laet/AFP/Getty Images; pp. 8–9 Everett Historical/Shutterstock.com; p. 11 Mohamed Abdulraheem/Shutterstock.com; p. 12 Dogora Sun/Shutterstock.com; p. 13 FloridaStock/Shutterstock.com; p. 15 zeljkosantrac/iStock/Getty Images; p. 16 Sean Pavone/iStock/Getty Images; p. 17 Shane Gross/Shutterstock.com; p. 18 Joecho-16/iStock/Getty Images; p. 19 a4ndreas/Shutterstock.com; p. 21 Stephane Cardinale/Corbis/Getty Images; p. 22 chudakov2/iStock/Getty Images; p. 23 Elena Elisseeva/Shutterstock.com; p. 24 Idoho Statesman/Tribune News Service/Getty Images; p. 25 Graeme Sloan/AP Images; p. 27 Philip Rozenski/Shutterstock.com; p. 29 oneinchpunch/Shutterstock.com.

Library of Congress Cataloging-in-Publication Data

Names: Faust, Daniel R., author.
Title: Protecting Earth's land / Daniel R. Faust.
Description: New York : Rosen Publishing, 2022. | Series: Spotlight on
   global issues | Includes index.
Identifiers: LCCN 2020003502 | ISBN 9781725323544 (paperback) | ISBN
   9781725323575 (library binding) | ISBN 9781725323551 (6 pack)
Subjects: LCSH: Pollution--Juvenile literature. | Nature--Effect of human
   beings on--Juvenile literature. | Weather--Effect of human beings
   on--Juvenile literature. | Environmental disasters--Juvenile literature.
   | Climatic changes--Juvenile literature.
Classification: LCC TD176 .F38 2022 | DDC 363.73--dc23
LC record available at https://lccn.loc.gov/2020003502

Manufactured in the United States of America

Some of the images in this book illustrate individuals who are models. The depictions do not imply actual situations or events.

CPSIA Compliance Information: Batch #CSR22. For further information contact Rosen Publishing, New York, New York at 1-800-237-9932.

Find us on

CONTENTS

CHAPTER ONE

EARTH'S CHANGING
LANDSCAPE

In 1910, President William H. Taft sighed a bill creating Glacier National Park in Montana. At the time, the park was home to more than 100 glaciers. Today, there are fewer than 30 glaciers in Glacier National Park. Scientists predict that within another 30 years, almost all of the park's glaciers will have disappeared.

Why are the glaciers melting? In the last decade, scientists have documented record-breaking high temperatures around the world. This global warming trend is one sign of the impact that humans are having on the planet. Scientists see disappearing glaciers as evidence of climate change.

Glaciers are an important natural resource. About two-thirds of our planet's fresh water is stored in glaciers. When the ice and snow melt, the water is released into rivers, streams, and oceans. As the glaciers at Earth's North and South Poles continue to melt, scientists predict that this additional water could cause sea levels around the world to rise as much as 200 feet (61 m). As sea levels rise, coastal areas could flood. With eight of the world's 10 largest cities built on or near the coast, rising sea levels could put billions of lives at risk.

The loss of glaciers is just one way human activities are damaging the planet. But there's hope. The actions of everyday people can help curb the harmful effects of global warming and pollution. Earth is our home, and we're all responsible for protecting it.

Bréf til framtíðarinnar

Ok er fyrsti nafnkunni jökullinn til að missa titil sinn.
Á næstu 200 árum er talið að allir jöklar landsins fari sömu leið.
Þetta minnismerki er til vitnis um að við vitum
hvað er að gerast og hvað þarf að gera.
Aðeins þú veist hvort við gerðum eitthvað.

A letter to the future

Ok is the first Icelandic glacier to lose its status as a glacier.
In the next 200 years all our glaciers are expected to follow the same path.
This monument is to acknowledge that we know
what is happening and what needs to be done.
Only you know if we did it.

Ágúst 2019
415ppm CO₂

Okjokull (Ok) glacier in Iceland once covered 6 square miles (9.6 square km) of land, but it melted so much that it was declared dead. This plaque marks where the glacier once stood.

CHAPTER TWO

DEVASTATING
DEFORESTATION

Forests cover about one-third of Earth's land. They provide food and shelter for countless species. Trees produce much of the planet's oxygen while absorbing much of the carbon dioxide that contributes to the greenhouse effect. They also provide shade that protects smaller plant species from the harmful effects of the sun.

Forests are an important resource for humans. We use wood from trees to build our homes. We eat the fruits and nuts that they grow. We use some plants and trees to make medicines. There are countless species found in the tropical rain forests of Africa and South America that people use to make drugs to treat heart disease, HIV, and some forms of cancer.

In 2019, the world watched as much of the Amazon rain forest burned. The fires, believed to have been set in order to clear land for use by people, drew the attention of activists and politicians around the world.

Unfortunately, people have also destroyed large sections of forest to make room for houses, farms, and cattle ranches. From the 1600s to the late 1800s, people cut down about half the forests in eastern North America. In South America, more than 20 percent of the Amazon rain forest has been destroyed.

Global warming is one of the more immediate effects of the destruction of Earth's forests. Fewer trees means more carbon dioxide in Earth's atmosphere. Carbon dioxide is a greenhouse gas that holds in heat from the sun, causing rising temperatures around the world. Forests also provide habitats for many living things. Destroying them may lead to species becoming endangered or extinct. Trees help absorb water before it reaches rivers and other bodies of water, preventing floods during heavy rain. They also help stabilize the soil, which reduces landslides.

Natural processes such as weathering, erosion, and deposition are all part of the planet's natural cycles. Weathering is the breaking down of rocks, minerals, and soil. Erosion involves the transportation of rocks and minerals from one place to another. Deposition is when these materials are left behind someplace else. The forces of water and wind carry out these processes naturally. Plants and trees slow erosion, trapping pieces of rocks and soil in their roots and preventing them from being washed away.

However, deforestation and other human activities are causing erosion to occur at an unnaturally rapid rate. Agriculture has caused about 80 percent of tropical deforestation around the world. Logging is also a big reason behind deforestation.

During the 1930s, thousands of families were forced to leave their farms on the Great Plains. Heavy winds created dust storms, blowing eroded soil over the land.

Agriculture also removes nutrients from soil. In the wild, nutrients are returned to the soil as dead plants and animals break down. But if a farmer uses the same field over and over, the soil will eventually run out of nutrients and become useless. When this happens, people often clear wild spaces and turn them into more farmland. Empty fields are left exposed to wind and rain. The loose dirt and soil is washed and blown away. This can lead to the collapse of entire ecosystems and create dust bowls.

A dust bowl is an area of land that suffers from dust storms and droughts, or long dry spells. During the 1930s, overfarming and other poor farming practices created a widespread dust bowl across the U.S. Great Plains. Today, land degradation has reduced the productivity of land across the globe by 23 percent.

CHAPTER THREE

RISING POPULATIONS, DISAPPEARING SPECIES

In 2019, a United Nations report estimated that three-quarters of land environments and about 66 percent of marine environments have been "significantly altered" by human actions.

Given that, perhaps the greatest threat that humans pose to the environment is overpopulation. As of December 2019, there were about 7.8 billion people living in the world, with more people being born every minute. Our planet is rapidly approaching the maximum population that our environment can sustain. As the human population increases, people use more natural resources, including animals, than Earth can replenish.

The earliest people were hunters and gatherers. People hunted animals for their meat, but they also used the animals' fur, skin, and bones to make clothing, tools, and shelter. However, as the human population grew, needed more resources, and created new weapons, people started killing animals faster than they could reproduce.

Today, overfishing also puts pressure on ocean species. Seafood is a dietary staple for about 3 billion people around the world. But poorly enforced rules and harmful commercial fishing practices are driving some species into extinction. Overfishing is damaging to marine ecosystems, which has a ripple effect and affects other systems.

Oceans cover about 70 percent of Earth's surface, and plants within their waters produce over half of the world's oxygen. At least 15 percent of earth's species live in the ocean. However, overfishing can put the balance of these natural systems at risk. It can harm not only the animals but also the plants and the environment around them.

Endangered sea turtles often die as part of bycatch—the accidental capture of unwanted sea creatures while fishing for different species.

Species with land habitats are also put at risk by rising populations. As noted earlier, one of the major effects of overpopulation is the destruction of wilderness areas to be used as farmland. People also clear large areas of natural wilderness to build towns and cities. Since 1992, urban, or city, areas have more than doubled throughout the world.

This can bring cities—and their residents—into greater contact with animals that live in the surrounding areas or that have adapted to life in urban areas. This can result in conflict. For example, farmers in Africa often kill cheetahs and hyenas, seeing them as pests. People also introduce invasive, or non-native, species to habitats. These species may prey on or compete with native species and drive them out.

Deforestation has more widespread consequences. Beyond changing or destroying the habitats where forests once stood, it contributes to global climate change, as there are fewer trees to absorb carbon dioxide. Deforestation affects ecosystems worldwide and puts pressure on wildlife.

As habitats change, species that are unable to adapt will die out.

The Arctic region is considered ground zero for climate change. This region is warming faster than anywhere else on the planet, causing snow, sea ice, and glaciers to melt. Arctic species, such as polar bears, are directly affected by global warming and Earth's changing land. Polar bears need sea ice to hunt and may starve without it. Walruses, seals, Arctic foxes, and narwhals are also affected by disappearing sea ice. If action isn't taken to curb the harmful effects of global warming, these species (and many others) may disappear from Earth forever.

CHAPTER FOUR

FALLING RESOURCES, RISING POLLUTION

People often rely on fossil fuels such as coal, oil, and natural gas to warm our houses, fuel our cars, and provide electricity. Not only do these fuels release harmful chemicals into the environment when they're burned, but they're also nonrenewable resources. That means once they've been used, there will be no way to replace them.

Because fossil fuels can only be found deep underground, the only way to reach them is to mine or drill into Earth's surface. One method of drilling for fossil fuels is called hydraulic fracturing. Hydraulic fracturing, or fracking, combines chemicals, sand, and large amounts of water and shoots them into the ground. The high-pressure stream of liquid and gas breaks up the rock surrounding oil and gas deposits. Fracking is potentially harmful for a number of reasons. First, it uses a great deal of water. Second, fracking releases dangerous pollutants into the air and water.

Everyday people contribute to pollution as well. The average person in the United States generates about five pounds (2.3 kg) of trash each day. That trash must go somewhere. Less than 25 percent of it is recycled, and the rest goes to dumps and landfills. A dump is a spot or hole in the ground where trash is buried. A landfill is a large structure built to contain trash and keep it away from the surrounding environment. Even though landfills are built to contain trash, toxins from their contents can still leach into the surrounding soil and water, harming local plant and animal species.

As of 2019, there were about 2,600 active landfills in the United States. Methane, a greenhouse gas, is the most common pollutant released by landfills.

CHAPTER FIVE

CHANGING
THE WATER CYCLE

Water is essential for life on Earth. All living things, from the tallest trees to the smallest bacteria, need water to survive. Humans are no different. But some people live in places where there isn't enough water. People build dams to block the flow of rivers and create man-made lakes called reservoirs. Reservoirs provide water for consumption, irrigation, recreation, and industrial use. Some dams use the flow of water to create electricity through hydroelectric generators. Lake Mead is a reservoir created by the Hoover Dam in the American Southwest. It provides water to Arizona, Nevada, California, and parts of Mexico.

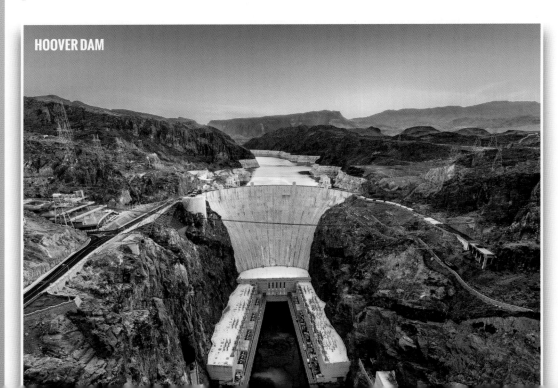

HOOVER DAM

The Great Pacific Garbage Patch is a collection of trash in the Pacific Ocean. There are nearly 2 trillion pieces of plastic floating in it.

By their very design, dams change the way rivers and other bodies of water function. Altering rivers, streams, and lakes can contribute to droughts and floods. A large dam can cause flooding in the surrounding area, destroying habitats. By blocking the flow of a river, dams can also create water shortages downriver. Without a steady supply of water, plants and animals in these areas could die out. Dams can also prevent fish from migrating, or moving from place to place. This limits their ability to find food and escape predators.

Water pollution is another serious impact that human activity has on the planet. Every year, over 8 million tons (7.2 mt) of garbage is dumped into the ocean. In addition, dangerous chemicals from fertilizers and pesticides often make their way into rivers and streams, poisoning local plants and animals.

CHAPTER SIX

MOVING
MOUNTAINS

Mountains are more than just a beautiful part of the landscape. Like everything else on Earth, mountains are an important part of the planet's natural cycles. The world's mountains are home to a wide range of ecosystems that support an incredibly diverse population of plant and animal species. Mountains also play a key role in the water cycle. Mountains force the air to flow high into the atmosphere, where the temperature is low enough that water vapor in the air creates clouds. Eventually, the clouds release this water as precipitation. Mountains also store water in a way. When it rains or snows near the chilly top of a mountain, the water collects as ice and snow. When the weather gets warmer, the ice and snow melt and flow downhill, feeding rivers, streams, and lakes.

Mountains play an important role in the Earth's water cycle. It's possible that destroying mountain environments could lead to the spread of desert environments.

Mountains are also a source of raw materials. Natural resources such as timber, iron, and coal can all be found in mountain environments. Humans have been digging mines into the sides of mountains for thousands of years. Mining can potentially change many things about a mountain and drastically affect the environment. Changing the shape of a mountain can prevent water from reaching lakes and rivers. Removing trees from mountain environments can lead to devastating landslides and destroy the natural habitats of many species. If mountains are changed too much, it can affect precipitation in the area and have a serious impact on the amount of rain that falls there, leading to droughts.

CHAPTER SEVEN

ACT NOW!

How much change is too much? Increasingly, there's been concern about how little natural land remains untouched by human activity. There's been a greater push to protect Earth's land through conservation.

Conserving land means protecting it and sometimes returning developed land to its natural state. Preserving the environment means that land and its natural resources should be maintained in their original, untouched state. The idea is that the value of land doesn't come from what you can take from it. It can still be enjoyed for and in its own natural state. This means these areas of land would no longer be available for many human uses, including mining, logging, or drilling.

Since 2017, there have been a number of changes to environmental regulations in the United States. Some land once protected by federal law will now be open to mining, logging, drilling, and cattle grazing. In 2019, the federal government announced a plan to allow oil drilling in Alaska's Arctic National Wildlife Refuge.

Many feel strongly that rolling back environmental protections to further pollute the environment is shortsighted and dangerous. Feeling that world leaders are failing, many young people are stepping up to protect Earth.

At age 15, Jamie Margolin decided that enough was enough. She and other young people couldn't wait for adults to take action to protect the environment and conserve natural resources. Together with her friend Nadia Nazar, she founded an organization called Zero Hour. This organization fights for climate and environmental justice, stressing that now is the time to act.

Margolin, shown here at the 2019 MTV EMAs in Seville, Spain, started Zero Hour in 2017.

Restoration is the process of returning developed or damaged ecosystems to their original natural state. Restoration involves studying the current environment and determining what the environment was like before humans changed it.

Wetlands, such as the Florida Everglades in the United States, are important ecosystems that serve as a link between the land and the water. Many species of plants and animals live in wetland habitats. Wetlands also provide a natural defense against flooding and storm damage and help control shoreline erosion. However, wetlands have also been an easy target for developers, farmers, and ranchers. Wetlands are being drained and destroyed faster than any other ecosystem. Activists are working to restore our nation's wetlands to their original state. This involves adding native plants, reintroducing native animal species, and restoring natural waterways.

Refitting buildings to use solar energy is a form of mitigation. Solar panels are a clean, renewable energy technology.

Remediation is the process of cleaning a contaminated area. The main goal is to clean and restore the area while causing as little harm as possible. One form of remediation is bioremediation, which uses naturally occurring organisms to break down pollutants into harmless substances. In 2010, bacteria were used to help clean up the Deepwater Horizon oil spill in the Gulf of Mexico.

Finally, environmental mitigation is any action or activity that's intended to remedy, reduce, or offset negative impacts to the environment caused by humans. Mitigation may include recycling items, planting trees, adopting renewable sources of energy, and making buildings more energy efficient.

CHAPTER EIGHT

EARTH DAY
AND GOING GREEN

Earth Day celebrated its 50th anniversary in 2020. The first Earth Day was organized by Senator Gaylord Nelson of Wisconsin and took place on April 22, 1970. Nelson was inspired to create the event after he witnessed the ecological destruction caused by an oil spill in Santa Barbara, California. Environmental awareness was already on the rise because of the 1962 publication of *Silent Spring* by Rachel Carson. The book, which detailed the effects of pesticides on the environment, became a best seller and raised public awareness of environmental issues.

On April 22, 1970, roughly 20 million Americans celebrated Earth Day by taking part in rallies for a healthy, sustainable environment. This first Earth Day is often considered the birth of the modern environmental movement. By the end of the 1970s, the United States government had passed the Clean Air Act, the Clean Water Act, and the Endangered Species Act. In 1990, on its 20th anniversary, Earth Day went global, with 200 million people holding demonstrations in 141 countries.

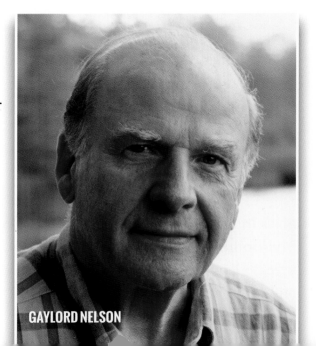

GAYLORD NELSON

FUTURE
THE HANDS
PRESIDENT WHO
D SCIENCE

I ...se to bring
a chi... into a
worl... with n...
fut...

When he was a teenager, Jerome Foster II founded OneMillionOfUs, an organization that raises awareness about climate change and other major social issues.

One of the results of Earth Day and the creation of the environmental movement was that many people became more aware of the impact that human activity has on the planet. More people started making an effort to live sustainably, which means living in a way that reduces their impact on the environment. One of the simplest ways to live sustainably is by reusing and recycling items whenever possible. Reusing and recycling reduces the amount of trash that we produce, which means we need to use less land for landfills.

In January 1970, the National Environmental Policy Act (NEPA) was signed into law. NEPA requires all federal agencies to assess the environmental impact of any proposed actions. It sets a process within which the agencies need to study any potential environmental (and related social or economic) effects.

Three major environmental protection laws followed in the United States. The Clean Air Act (CAA) of 1970 was passed to work toward preventing air pollution and protecting the ozone layer. The CAA gave the Environmental Protection Agency (EPA) the power to fight environmental pollution. It also established national guidelines for regulating and enforcing air quality standards. The Clean Water Act of 1972 set standards and regulations intended to restore and maintain clean and healthy water. In addition to fighting water pollution, the Clean Water Act also addressed environmental issues such as the protection of U.S. wetlands.

The Endangered Species Act (ESA) of 1973 gave the federal government the authority to protect endangered and threatened species and the habitats they call home. The ESA creates lists of protected plant and animal species with the goal of restoring them to healthy populations.

However, recent changes to the ESA weaken the protections for endangered species and their habitats. Critics argue that these changes favor mining, drilling, and other commercial industries over the safety of protected species.

Created in 1970, the United States Environmental Protection Agency is a federal agency responsible for environmental study, research, and education. It's also responsible for enforcing federal environmental laws.

William Jefferson
Clinton Federal
Building

12th Street
NW
Entrance

U.S. Environmental
Protection Agency
(North and South
Entrances)

The environmental movement isn't limited to the United States. In 1972, the United Nations formed the United Nations Environment Programme (UNEP). UNEP has become the leading global authority on environmental issues. It provides leadership and encourages partnership in addressing environmental issues around the world. UNEP also helps developing countries put healthy environmental practices in place.

In 2016, many countries signed the UN's Paris Agreement. This is the world's first comprehensive global climate agreement. The main goal of the Paris Agreement is to address the role of human activity in climate change. The countries involved seek to keep the global temperature from rising more than 3.6°Fahrenheit (2°Celsius) from where it was before the Industrial Revolution. Under the agreement, each country commits to develop and implement plans to reduce and fight the effects of greenhouse gas emissions. The countries also agree to reduce their reliance on fossil fuels and to research new technologies that will help reduce their carbon footprint, or the amount of greenhouse gases (specifically carbon dioxide) they produce.

As of 2020, representatives of 197 countries have signed the Paris Agreement, with the last country being Syria. However, in 2017, U.S. President Donald Trump announced his intention of withdrawing the United States from the Paris Agreement. This was set to take place in November 2020.

Trump's decision was met with protest by environmental activists. Unless immediate action is taken, certain habitats may be unable to recover from the damage that climate change has already caused.

Saving the environment is a global issue. In recent years, activists around the world, many of them teenagers and young adults, have held rallies and protests in order to convince politicians of the importance of environmental issues.

OF
OLLUTION

THERE
IS NO
B

THIS IS
OUR HOME

CHAPTER NINE

WHAT CAN YOU DO?

Protecting Earth's land can sometimes feel overwhelming. But small changes can produce large results. Issues such as global warming, climate change, air pollution, and water pollution should concern everyone on the planet, regardless of age, race, gender, or economic class. It's up to all of us to do our part to help protect Earth's land.

Teenage activists are leading the charge in today's environmental movement. At the age of 12, Haven Coleman became a cofounder and codirector of the U.S. Youth Climate Strike, which organizes weekly school strikes to demand politicians take action to save the environment. Climate activist Eyal Weintraub of Argentina was a teenager when he organized a protest in front of Argentina's national congress in Buenos Aires. These young activists use protests, marches, speeches, sit-ins, and social media to make their voices heard.

You can use social media to add your voice to theirs. Posting videos of you and your friends cleaning a local park or planting trees can inspire others to do the same. Signing online petitions and tweeting your local politicians are also great ways to make your voice heard. Ask your teachers if you can hold a rally at your school to promote environmental causes or hold fundraisers to raise money for organizations fighting to save the planet. The future belongs to you and your friends, and you have every right to speak up and demand that you inherit a clean and healthy Earth.

GLOSSARY

activist (AK-tih-vist) Someone who acts strongly in support of or against an issue.

cancer (KAN-suhr) A disease caused by the uncontrolled growth of cells in the body.

comprehensive (kahm-pri-HEN-siv) Including many, most, or all things.

document (DAH-kyuh-muhnt) To create a record of something.

efficient (ih-FIH-shuhnt) Done in the quickest, best way possible.

fossil fuel (FAH-suhl FYOOL) A fuel—such as coal, oil, or natural gas—that is formed in the earth from dead plants or animals.

greenhouse effect (GREEN-howz ih-FEKT) The warming of Earth's atmosphere due to gases that trap energy from the sun.

greenhouse gas (GREEN-howz GASS) A gas in the atmosphere that traps energy from the sun.

HIV (AYCH-EYE-VEE) Human immunodeficiency virus, an illness that interferes with the body's ability to fight infections.

irrigation (eer-uh-GAY-shuhn) The supplying of water to land by man-made means.

leach (LEECH) To draw out or leak out.

nutrient (NOO-tree-uhnt) Something taken in by a plant or animal that helps it grow and stay healthy.

pesticide (PEH-stuh-syd) A poison used to kill pests.

precipitation (prih-sih-puh-TAY-shuhn) Water that falls to the ground as hail, mist, rain, sleet, or snow.

sustain (suh-STAIN) To provide what is needed for someone or something to exist.

technology (tek-NAH-luh-jee) A method that uses science to solve problems and the tools used to solve those problems.

INDEX

PRIMARY SOURCE LIST

Page 5
Plaque placed at the former location of Icelandic Okjokull glacier. Photograph. July 18, 2019. Iceland. Held by Wikimedia Commons.

Page 7
Forest fires in Brazil. Photograph. August 27, 2019. By Joao Laet. Held by Getty Images.

Page 9
Machinery buried by dust storms. Photograph. 1936. Dallas, South Dakota. Now kept at Everett Historical.

WEBSITES

Due to the changing nature of Internet links, Rosen Publishing has developed an online list of websites related to the subject of this book. This site is updated regularly. Please use this link to access the list: www.powerkidslinks.com/SOGI/earthsland